976.2
WAT
Watson, Galadriel Findlay
North Dakota
34880000 823141

NORTH DAKOTA

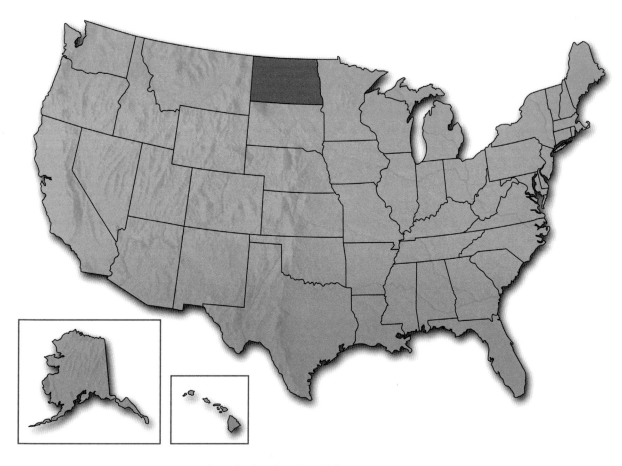

Galadriel Findlay Watson

Published by Weigl Publishers Inc.
123 South Broad Street, Box 227
Mankato, MN 56002
USA
Web site: http://www.weigl.com

Library of Congress Cataloging-in-Publication Data

Watson, Galadriel Findlay.
    North Dakota / Galadriel Findlay Watson.
        p. cm. -- (A kid's guide to American states)
    Includes index.
    ISBN 1-930954-53-0 (lib. bdg.)
    1. North Dakota--Juvenile literature. [1. North Dakota.] I. Title. II. Series.

F636.3 . W38 2001

2001017993

ISBN 1-930954-96-4 (pbk.)

Printed in the United States of America
1 2 3 4 5 6 7 8 9 10   05 04 03 02 01

Project Coordinator
Michael Lowry
Substantive Editor
Jennifer Nault
Copy Editor
Bryan Pezzi
Designers
Warren Clark
Terry Paulhus
Layout
Susan Kenyon
Photo Researcher
Diana Marshall

Photograph Credits
Every reasonable effort has been made to trace ownership and to obtain
permission to reprint copyright material. The publishers would be
pleased to have any errors or omissions brought to their attention so
that they may be corrected in subsequent printings.

Cover: Native American beadwork (PhotoSpin, Inc.), Prairie grass (Steve Mulligan);
Archive Photos: page 24BL; **Bismark-Mandan Convention & Visitors Bureau:** pages
4BR, 21T, 29TR; **Mike Copeman/Courtesy Northlands Park:** page 26T; **Corel
Corporation:** page 28BL; **Corbis Corporation:** pages 27T, 27B; **Craig Bihrle/North
Dakota Game and Fish Department:** pages 3T, 3M, 5BL, 6T, 6B, 8T, 9BL, 9BR, 10BR;
Dakota Dinosaur Museum: page 25T; **Defense Visual Information Center:** page 15B;
Digital Stock Corporation: page 29TL; **Digital Vision:** page 20B; **Eric R. Berndt/The
Image Finders:** page 9T; **Fargo-Moorhead Convention & Visitors Bureau:** page 20T;
Mark E. Gibson/The Image Finders: page 15T; **International Music Camp:** page
24BR; **Jamestown Promotion and Tourism Center:** pages 10BL, 12BL; **Lampo
Communications:** page 14BL; **Steve Mulligan:** pages 8B, 12BR; **North Dakota
Tourism Department:** pages 3B, 4T, 4BL, 5T, 7T, 7BL, 7BR, 10T, 11BL, 12T, 13T, 13B,
14T, 14BR, 16BL, 22T, 22B, 23B, 23T, 24T; **PhotoDisc, Inc.:** pages 21BL, 21BR, 28BR;
Photofest: pages 25B, 26B; **PhotoSpin, Inc.:** page 26BL; **State Historical Society of
North Dakota:** pages 16T, 16BR, 17T, 17B, 18T, 18BL, 18BR, 19T, 19B; **U.S. Fish &
Wildlife Service:** pages 11T, 11BR; **Marilyn "Angel" Wynn:** page 23M.

CONTENTS

Farmland covers 39.4 million acres of North Dakota.

INTRODUCTION

Stretching out beneath North Dakota's infinite skies, the wide open prairie offers the state's residents a comfortable place to call home. North Dakota is ranked the safest state in the country, having the lowest crime rate in the United States. North Dakota's vast plains contain some of the most abundant wheat fields in the nation, producing enough wheat in one year to make 108 billion sandwiches. Agriculture accounts for more than 37 percent of the state's economic base, making it North Dakota's number one industry. Much of the nation's wheat, barley, sunflowers, and flaxseed are provided by the hard work of North Dakota farmers.

North Dakota is gaining a reputation as a tourist destination, bringing in more than 3 million visitors to the state each year. A rich Native-American heritage, enlightening historic sites, and beautiful state parks attract many travelers from all over the world.

Fort Abraham Lincoln was where General George Custer commanded the 7th Cavalry, before they rode out to encounter the Sioux at Little Big Horn.

QUICK FACTS

The state song, the "North Dakota Hymn," was first performed in public in 1927. It was officially adopted twenty years later.

The state seal contains forty-two stars, which represent the number of states in the Union after North Dakota, South Dakota, Montana, and Washington were admitted in 1889.

The state flag was adopted in 1911. It shows a bald eagle holding seven arrows in one talon and an olive branch with three red berries in the other.

More than 87,000 miles of roads and highways crisscross North Dakota.

Getting There

North Dakota is located in the northcentral part of the United States. It is bordered by Minnesota to the east, South Dakota to the south, Montana to the west, and Canada to the north. North Dakota sits exactly in the middle of the North American continent. A monument in the town of Rugby marks what is believed to be the continent's **geographic** center.

About 420 municipal and private airports serve North Dakota. The busiest airport is in Fargo. Passenger trains travel through several North Dakota cities, and there are about a dozen bus lines offering scheduled and chartered services. Visitors driving to North Dakota have access to two interstate highways and seven United States highways. For those travelers heading east or west, the main highway is Interstate 94. Interstate 29 is the primary north-south route.

QUICK FACTS

Teredo petrified wood is the state **fossil**.

The state motto is "Liberty and Union Now and Forever, One and Inseparable."

North Dakota is the seventeenth-largest state in the country. It covers 70,704 square miles of land.

North Dakota's state bird is the western meadowlark.

North Dakota Location Map

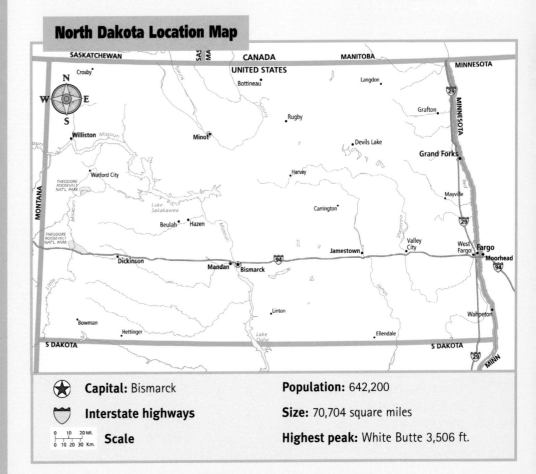

⭐ **Capital:** Bismarck

🛡 **Interstate highways**

Scale 0 10 20 MI. 0 10 20 30 Km.

Population: 642,200

Size: 70,704 square miles

Highest peak: White Butte 3,506 ft.

Bismarck was named in honor of Prince Otto Von Bismarck of Germany.

QUICK FACTS

The name "Dakota" means "allies" or "friends." The term comes from the Dakota people, who were also known as the Sioux.

Bismarck is the state capital. The city also served as the capital of the Dakota Territory from 1883 to 1889.

The state march is the "Flickertail March." It was once called "Spirit of the Land," until it was discovered that another march had a similar title.

In 1803, the United States bought the northwest half of what is now North Dakota from France, as a part of the **Louisiana Purchase**. The southeast half was obtained through a border treaty with Britain in 1818.

Native Americans were the first people to inhabit the area now called North Dakota. Explorers and fur traders arrived next, establishing the first permanent European settlements in the region. North Dakota's geographic isolation has kept the state's population low. Today, North Dakota still has one of the lowest populations in the country.

North Dakota was initially part of the Dakota Territory. This territory also included South Dakota, as well as parts of Montana and Wyoming. By the time the Dakota Territory became eligible for statehood, it was clear that the north and south had little in common. The railroad ran across the territory from east to west, and people living in the north rarely interacted with people in the south. Each region wanted its own government. On November 2, 1889, North Dakota and South Dakota were admitted to the Union as separate states.

Lake Sakakawea is named in honor of Sacagawea, the Shoshone woman who helped lead Meriwether Lewis and William Clark on their journey to find a waterway to the Pacific Ocean.

Medora's Old West Cowboy Town draws in 500,000 tourists each year. Medora is home to about 100 residents.

North Dakotans are proud of their culture and heritage. Many festivals honor pioneer life and the culture of the early European settlers. Native Peoples celebrate their culture through **powwows**. Many of North Dakota's residents enjoy fairs, theater productions, and symphonies. Sports, such as basketball, snowmobiling, and fishing, are also popular.

Each one of North Dakota's many nicknames highlights a different aspect of the state. "The Sioux State" refers to North Dakota's Native-American heritage, while "The Flickertail State" comes from the flickertail squirrel, which is common throughout the state. "The Roughrider State" refers to the First United States Volunteer Cavalry, which fought in the Spanish-American War under the leadership of North Dakotan Theodore Roosevelt. The nickname written on North Dakota license plates, "The Peace Garden State," refers to the state's International Peace Garden.

QUICK FACTS

Residents of North Dakota are sometimes called Roughriders, after one of the state's nicknames.

Westhope, on US Highway 83, is the busiest entry into Canada. Over 72,000 vehicles cross its border every year.

North Dakota has six state universities. The oldest is the University of North Dakota, which was founded in 1883 at Grand Forks.

University of North Dakota

The International Peace Garden straddles the border with Canada and stands as a symbol of peace between the two countries. It covers 888 acres of land in the United States and 1,451 acres of land in Canada.

The coldest temperature ever recorded in North Dakota was –60˚F. It occurred on February 15, 1936, in Parshall.

LAND AND CLIMATE

North Dakota has long, cold winters and short, hot summers. It is one of the driest states in the country. Some areas in the west receive only 13 inches of rain or snow each year. The state's average **precipitation** is 17 inches per year—much less than the national average of 30 inches per year. Temperatures average 70˚ Fahrenheit in the summer and 7˚F in the winter. Chinooks often sweep over the state. These warm, westerly winds quickly boost winter temperatures.

North Dakota is divided into three geographic regions. In the west, there is an area of high, level ground called the Missouri Plateau. With very little rain in the region, farming is nearly impossible. In the center of the state is the Drift Prairie region. This gently rolling plain is covered with **pothole lakes**. The rich soil is ideal farmland. In the east is the Red River Valley. This region was once covered by a large lake, which had formed from glacial meltwater. When the lake dried, it left behind a treeless, flat land with rich soils—also perfect for farming.

The term badlands was coined by early travelers who found the hills "bad lands" to travel through.

NATURAL RESOURCES

North Dakota's most important natural resource is its soil. In the Drift Prairie and Red River Valley regions, melting glaciers left behind layers of drift. This was a mixture of clay, sand, **humus**, and gravel that combined over time to form rich, dark soil.

Oil is North Dakota's second-most important resource. Oil was discovered in the northwest in 1951. Seventeen of the state's western counties contain oil fields. Many of North Dakota's oil deposits are found in the Williston Basin, a vast natural structure that runs beneath the state.

North Dakota contains large deposits of coal. The state produces about 30 million tons of coal yearly. Coal is generated into electric power at eight different plants in the state.

North Dakota farmland would cover 12 million city blocks.

QUICK FACTS

North Dakota has the largest deposit of **lignite coal** in the United States.

Other natural resources in North Dakota include clay, sand, gravel, and salt. A small amount of lumber is produced in the Turtle Mountains, the Pembina Hills, and the hills around Devils Lake.

North Dakota's approximately 600 dams control floods, supply water for drinking and crop irrigation, and generate electricity.

About two-thirds of the nation's lignite coal can be found in western North Dakota.

The wild prairie rose is the state flower. It grows along roadsides, in pastures, and in meadows.

PLANTS AND ANIMALS

In the summer, North Dakota's prairies are covered with flowers such as pasqueflowers, black-eyed Susans, red lilies, and wild prairie roses. Berry pickers can find chokecherries, highbush cranberries, and wild plums.

There are very few trees in North Dakota. In fact, less than 1 percent of the state is forested. The Turtle Mountain region, in the northern part of the state, is one of the few wooded areas. The state tree, the American elm, is found across the state, and can grow over 120 feet tall.

North Dakota's **wetlands** provide food and shelter for birds and animals. Wetlands once covered nearly two-thirds of the entire state. Now, more than half of this area is gone. Much of the wetlands were drained or filled to grow crops and allow for the construction of buildings. The remaining wetlands are found mostly north and east of the Missouri River.

North Dakota's western plains provide an ideal habitat for the black-tailed prairie dog.

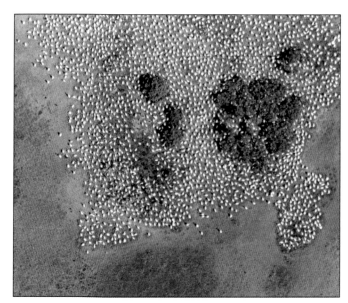

Between 10,000 and 12,000 white pelicans live at the Chase Lake National Wildlife Refuge.

North Dakota is home to many types of animals. White-tailed deer live throughout the state, while prairie dogs, mule deer, and pronghorn antelopes roam the badlands. Badgers, beavers, bobcats, and coyotes are also common in North Dakota. The flickertail squirrel, also called the Richardson's ground squirrel, makes its home in the central part of the state.

Nearly 400 species of birds can be found in North Dakota. Chase Lake National Wildlife Refuge, near Medina, is the largest pelican breeding colony in North America. The state also has a large duck population. More ducks hatch in North Dakota than in any other state except Alaska. Every year, 2 to 3 million ducklings hatch in the Peace Garden State. About 100 whooping cranes, the tallest bird in North America, **migrate** across the state in spring and fall.

North Dakota's waters are home to sixty species of fish, catfish, trout, perch, and bass. There are two federal fish hatcheries in North Dakota, which stock nearly 200 lakes and rivers. As for reptiles, there are frogs, toads, turtles, and snakes—including the poisonous prairie rattlesnake.

QUICK FACTS

Huge herds of bison once roamed the state, but most were killed by hunters in the 1800s. Today, bison numbers have increased to 15,000. They live on private ranches, game preserves, and in parks.

The state fish is the northern pike, and the state horse is the nokota. North Dakota even has a state grass—the western wheatgrass.

Elk, deer, bison, and waterfowl can be found at Sully's Hill National Game Preserve.

Elk

White pelicans have a wing span of up to 9 feet.

Theodore Roosevelt's log cabin in North Dakota is open to visitors. Roosevelt owned two large ranches in the state.

QUICK FACTS

Theodore Roosevelt National Park was named after the twenty-sixth president of the United States. Roosevelt was a rancher in North Dakota for several years. In 1886, he returned to politics in New York.

The International Peace Garden hosts the annual International Music Camp, one of North America's finest summer schools for the arts.

The world's largest bison statue is in Jamestown. It is 26 feet high and weighs 60 tons.

TOURISM

North Dakota's natural rugged beauty is an important draw for the state's tourism industry. Visitors to the state can explore more than a dozen state parks and recreational areas, as well as several state forests and national grasslands. North Dakota's only national park is Theodore Roosevelt National Park, near Medora. Located in the northern part of the state, the International Peace Garden attracts more than 250,000 visitors each year.

North Dakota is also home to many historical attractions. Tourists can walk through a restored pioneer town at Bonanzaville in Fargo or visit Fort Abercrombie, which in 1857 became the first United States military post in North Dakota. Visitors can follow the footsteps of explorers Lewis and Clark by taking a 300-mile drive along the banks of the Missouri River. The drive includes stops at a re-creation of Fort Mandan and at the Knife River Indian Villages National Historic Site.

The Theodore Roosevelt National Park is a breathtaking 70,448-acre wildlife preserve in western North Dakota.

INDUSTRY

More than 90 percent of North Dakota's electric power is provided by steam plants that burn the state's coal.

North Dakota's industry is dominated by agriculture, followed by mining, manufacturing, and tourism. With such fertile soil, farming is more important to North Dakota than to most other states. More than 30,000 farms and ranches cover 90 percent of the state.

In 1884, the Northern Pacific Railroad began mining along its railroad tracks. This was the start of North Dakota's coal-mining industry. Today, lignite coal is mined throughout the state. Because lignite coal is found close to the surface, it is easy to mine.

Oil from western North Dakota is processed at an oil refinery in Mandan. Many people are employed to drill for oil, and clean and refine it.

Most of the state's manufacturing is based on the processing of raw materials from the state's farms and mines. Wheat is made into breads and pastas, milk is used for cheeses, and sugar is extracted from sugar beets. Meat-packing plants produce steaks and sausages.

QUICK FACTS

A plant in Rolla makes **bearings** for the United States military from artificial rubies and sapphires.

Some plants in North Dakota make newspaper, aircraft parts, wood cabinets, and furniture.

About 6 percent of North Dakotans work in the manufacturing industry.

The pumps that remove oil from the ground are called "nodding donkeys."

Wheat and wheat products are North Dakota's number one agricultural export.

GOODS AND SERVICES

North Dakota is a leading producer of many food crops. Crops are grown mainly in the Drift Prairie and Red River Valley regions, in the central and eastern parts of the state. Wheat is the state's most important product. Only Kansas grows more wheat than North Dakota. The state is the nation's leading producer of durum wheat, which is used to make pasta. It is also the country's number one producer of barley, sunflowers, and flaxseed. North Dakota produces more pinto beans, rye, and oats than any other state. The state's sugar beets provide much of the nation's sugar, while its potatoes are made into potato chips and flakes for instant mashed potatoes.

Cattle are another important source of income for North Dakota. Cattle graze on ranches in the dry western part of the state. The cattle provide beef and dairy products. Hogs, poultry, and sheep are also raised.

North Dakota ranks first in the nation for the production of sunflowers.

North Dakotans can choose to read from almost 100 newspapers, including 10 daily newspapers.

A large majority of North Dakotans earn their income working in the service industry. Some are employed in businesses, such as banks, restaurants, stores, and tourist attractions. Others work for state and federal government services, such as the federal air force bases in Minot and Grand Forks. The bases were built to defend the country during the Cold War. The Minot Air Force Base employs 4,800 military personnel and 1,200 civilian workers. Employment can also be found in the state's transportation, communication, and utility sectors.

QUICK FACTS

The prices of wheat and oil can vary greatly. Price reductions have a dramatic effect on the state's income. North Dakota leaders formed the Vision 2000 Committee to find new ways to maintain the economy.

If North Dakota were a country, it would be among the world's top nuclear powers, because of its many nuclear missiles.

North Dakota's news media keeps the state's residents abreast of current affairs. North Dakota's daily newspapers with the largest circulation are the *Bismarck Tribune*, the *Fargo Forum*, the *Grand Forks Herald* and the *Minot Daily News*. There are also many locally-published magazines and dozens of television and radio stations.

The Minot Air Force Base is one of three operational missile units in the United States. The base houses 150 nuclear missiles, which are contained in underground silos spread across 8,500 squares miles of land.

The Sioux, or Dakota, lived in the southwestern part of North Dakota.

FIRST NATIONS

The Woodland culture was the first group of people to settle in what is now North Dakota. In 400 BC, the Woodland could be found living in villages along North Dakota's rivers. They hunted animals for meat, and grew corn and squash. Around 600 AD, bison hunters came to the North Dakota area. They lived in tepees and were always on the move as they followed the bison herds.

By the seventeenth century, Native-American groups began to settle near the Missouri River. These groups included the Mandan, Hidatsa, and Arikara. They built permanent villages, hunted bison, and farmed the land.

Beginning in the late seventeenth century, other Native Peoples began arriving in North Dakota. The Dakota, or Sioux, came from central Minnesota and settled in the Drift Prairie region. The Ojibwa, also from Minnesota, moved into the forests of the Turtle and Pembina Mountains of the northeast. These groups remained in the area until conflicts over land developed with the United States government during the last half of the nineteenth century.

The Dakota were the largest Native-American group in North Dakota.

Catholic missionary Father George Anthony Belcourt built the state's first flour mill at St. Joseph in 1851.

QUICK FACTS

In 1797, David Thompson became the first **surveyor** to chart part of North Dakota. He is also the first European to see Turtle Lake, one of the sources of the Mississippi River.

More than 11,000 furs were traded in the lower Red River Valley during the 1804–1805 season.

The piles of rock on North Dakota's highest point, White Butte, are called "johnnies" or "sheepherder's monuments." Many people believe that these rocks were piled there by sheepherders, as a way to pass the time while tending their flocks.

The town of Minot was founded in the late 1800s, and named after Henry D. Minot, a young entrepreneur from the east. Minot was nicknamed the "Magic City" because of its phenomenal early growth.

EXPLORERS AND MISSIONARIES

In 1738, Pierre Gaultier de Varennes, Sieur de La Vérendrye, became the first person of European heritage to visit what is now North Dakota. This French-Canadian fur trader was followed by other fur traders from England, France, and Spain. The fur trade was soon under the control of two British-owned companies—the North West Company and the Hudson's Bay Company. In 1801, the first permanent trading post in North Dakota was established at Pembina, by Alexander Henry the Younger.

A small number of missionaries also ventured into the area. The first of these was Catholic Father Sévère Dumoulin, who built a chapel at Pembina in 1818. That same year, Father Joseph Provencher started a mission at Fort Douglas.

The first school in North Dakota was opened in Pembina, in 1818, by Catholic missionaries.

North Dakota's settlers often built their homes out of sod. Sod houses provided excellent insulation from the prairie winds.

EARLY SETTLERS

In 1812, Scottish and Irish settlers came from Canada to start their own colony. Called the Selkirk Colony, this group lived at Pembina and grew food for fur trappers and traders. They also started North Dakota's first school. In 1823, the Selkirk Colony returned to Canada.

In 1861, the Dakota Territory was created. Even though Native Americans already lived in the area, it was opened up for **homesteading**. European settlers also began to kill large numbers of bison, which the Native Americans depended on for food. As settlement increased, conflicts arose between the new settlers and the Native Peoples. Eventually, the United States forced many Native Americans onto **reservations.**

QUICK FACTS

Since there were very few trees, settlers built houses using blocks of dirt and grass called sod.

Drought, prairie fires, and blizzards ravaged the area in 1886 and 1887. Many settlers died or moved away.

Bonanza farms first appeared in 1873. They were huge, profitable wheat farms that were run like factories. Most disappeared after wheat prices fell in 1890.

Scottish and Irish pioneers were the first European settlers in North Dakota.

After the railroad was built, stagecoaches were used mainly for express travel between towns without rail connections.

Many settlers were not willing to move to the new Dakota Territory because of the conflicts with the Native Peoples. Transportation was also a problem. While there were steamboats on the Missouri and Red Rivers, it was still a difficult journey by stagecoach or ox-drawn wagon, to get to any other part of the territory. When the first railroad came to the area in 1872, travel became much easier. By 1881, railroad tracks ran from one side of the Dakota Territory to the other.

As transportation improved, European settlement in the area began to grow. Many new settlers started their own small farms, growing mostly wheat. Others worked on the large bonanza farms. Most of the settlers were **immigrants** from countries such as Norway, Germany, and modern-day Czech Republic and Slovakia.

Between 1879 and 1886 more than 100,000 immigrants settled in North Dakota.

Fargo is North Dakota's largest city, with approximately 86,700 residents.

POPULATION

North Dakota is one of the least populated states in the country, with about 642,200 people. The population has decreased since 1920, when the state had about 647,000 residents. The state also has one of the lowest **population density** rates, with only about 9 people per square mile. The average population density for the United States is 77 people per square mile.

While only about 53 percent of North Dakota's population lives in **urban** areas, the state's population has been shifting over the years. As a result, North Dakota cities, while not large by national standards, are rapidly increasing in population. Between 1950 and 1990, Bismarck more than doubled its number of residents. At 54,040 people, it is the second largest city in the state. Grand Forks follows close behind with 47,327 people.

One-quarter of the population of North Dakota is under the age of 18.

With nineteen stories, the State Capitol in Bismarck is North Dakota's tallest building.

John Miller, a successful farmer and land investor, was North Dakota's first governor.

North Dakota is governed under its original constitution, which was adopted in 1889.

The state is divided into fifty-three counties.

North Dakota is the only state not to have voter registration.

Beryl Levine became the first woman Justice on North Dakota's Supreme Court in 1985.

North Dakota has seven judicial districts, which elect a total of forty-three district court judges.

POLITICS AND GOVERNMENT

The state's government is divided into three branches—the legislative, the executive, and the judicial. The legislative branch, called the Legislative Assembly, makes the laws. It is made up of forty-nine senators and ninety-eight members from the House of Representatives. Senators serve four-year terms, while house members serve two-year terms.

The executive branch carries out the laws. The governor is the chief executive and is elected for a four-year term. The state also has a lieutenant governor, elected officials, and **appointed** officials. North Dakota's **decentralized** method of governing gives each official authority over his or her own department.

The judicial branch interprets the laws by ruling on civil and criminal cases. The highest court is the Supreme Court, which is made up of five judges.

Judges in North Dakota are elected to six-year terms.

Fargo hosts the annual German Folk Festival in June.

CULTURAL GROUPS

Roughly 95 percent of North Dakota's residents can trace their roots back to European countries. Early Norwegians settled in the Red River Valley and northcentral North Dakota. Many Germans and Russians settled in the southcentral part of the state. By 1910, most residents in North Dakota were of European heritage. At the time, the state was home to more people that were born in other countries than any other state. North Dakota's European immigrants brought their religious beliefs with them. Today, 48 percent of North Dakotans are Lutheran, while another 38 percent are Roman Catholic.

Those of Scandinavian heritage celebrate their culture at Fargo's Scandinavian Festival. The event attracts members of the Norwegian royal family to North Dakota. German culture is honored at the state's numerous Oktoberfests.

QUICK FACTS

The town of New Leipzig is called "The Small, Friendly German Town on the Dakota Prairie." Each fall, it hosts a traditional German Oktoberfest.

The city of Minot is home to the Norsk Hostfest. It is North America's largest Scandinavian festival. The event features world-class entertainment and serves up Scandinavian foods and delicacies.

The German Folk Festival in Fargo is a celebration of German music, costumes, and food. The highlight of the event is the German brass band that plays traditional German tunes.

The first Norsk Hostfest was accidentally called Hostefest. "Hoste" means "cough," so the name, when translated meant "Coughing Festival."

The largest non-European cultural group is the state's Native Americans. More than one-third of the state's Native-American population lives on the Turtle Mountain Indian Reservation. The Mandan, the Hidatsa, and the Arikara live in Fort Berthold at Lake Sakakawea, while the Devils Lake Sioux live in Fort Totten, south of the lake. The Standing Rock Sioux live in Standing Rock along the South Dakota border.

The United Tribes International Powwow features some 1,500 dancers and drummers.

The United Tribes International Powwow is held each September at the Lone Star Arena in Bismarck. More than 20,000 visitors come to witness the dancing and singing competitions between members of North Dakota's Native-American communities. Nearly seventy First Nations groups are represented each year.

Sioux spirit dolls were made by mothers for their children. When the children were born they were given the same name as the doll.

The Trollwood Performing Arts School puts on full-length musicals each summer.

QUICK FACTS

North Dakota's oldest newspaper, the *Bismarck Tribune*, was started in 1873.

The state's universities and colleges are important cultural centers. North Dakota State University is home to the Reinecke Fine Arts Center.

The movie *Fargo* was filmed in North Dakota. *Fargo* won an Academy Award for best original screenplay and Frances McDormand won best actress.

ARTS AND ENTERTAINMENT

North Dakota holds dozens of festivals each year. The North Dakota State Fair at Minot is held the third week in July, and the Dakota Cowboy Poetry Gathering is held every Memorial Day in Medora. Minot's Winterfest happens in February, and the North Dakota Winter Show takes place in Valley City every March.

Music lovers can attend symphony orchestras in Minot, Fargo, and Grand Forks. The annual International Old-Time Fiddlers' Contest occurs at the International Peace Garden. Residents and visitors also enjoy the state's many museums, art galleries, zoos, and dance companies. The Children's Museum at Yunker Farm offers families a fun way to learn about nature and agriculture. Visitors can observe a display of live bees and crawl around in a giant honeycomb.

The International Peace Garden holds the annual International Old-Time Fiddlers' Contest. Competitions are held between musicians from all over North America.

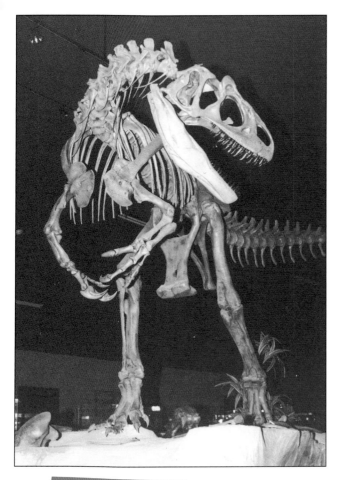

The 13,400-square-foot Dakota Dinosaur Museum is located in Dickinson.

Several well-known performers and artists have come from North Dakota. Angie Dickinson is an actor best known for her role on the 1970s television series *Police Woman*. Maxwell Anderson is a Pulitzer Prize winning playwright and graduate of the University of North Dakota. Louis L'Amour, a best-selling novelist, grew up in Jameston. Another Jamestown native was singer and actor Peggy Lee. Lee sang with Benny Goodman's band and with Bing Crosby. Bandleader Lawrence Welk was from North Dakota and hosted his own television program—*The Lawrence Welk Show*. Phyllis Frelich, an actor who is deaf, helped found the National Theatre of the Deaf. North Dakota's Richard Edlund has won several Academy Awards for his special effects in movies like *Poltergeist*, *Ghostbusters*, and *Fright Night*.

QUICK FACTS

Visitors to the Dakota Dinosaur Museum, in Dickinson, can view twelve full-scale dinosaur replicas. The museum's large collection of fossils started in 1984 when dinosaur remains were dug out of the ground in the Dickinson area.

Every year, the town of Turtle Lake hosts the United States's Turtle Racing Championship. Activities include a soap-box derby, a softball tournament, street dancing, and the turtle race itself.

Because so many residents live in the country or in small towns, many North Dakotans do not have access to libraries. The government is trying to solve this problem by opening more small libraries and by sending bookmobiles into remote areas.

For *Ghostbusters*, Richard Edlund created close to 200 difficult special-effects shots in less than one year.

The Killdeer Mountain Roundup Rodeo is North Dakota's oldest professional rodeo.

SPORTS

While there are no professional sports teams in North Dakota, residents enjoy watching college and high-school sports, especially basketball and football. These are covered by local radio and television stations.

North Dakota is host to many amateur sports events. The Prairie Rose State Games has events similar to the Olympics. Grand Forks' Potato Bowl USA is another popular event. It takes place in September and features a football game and a parade. The Great American Horse Race is held each September at Fort Abraham Lincoln State Park, and the town of Sentinel Butte hosts the Champions' Ride Rodeo every August.

Baseball great Roger Maris grew up in North Dakota. He was the American League's Most Valuable Player in the 1960–1961 season. In 1961, he broke the record for the most home runs hit in one season—sixty-one.

QUICK FACTS

The Fighting Sioux, the University of North Dakota's hockey team, has won seven national championships in the team's history.

Boxer Virgil Hill grew up in North Dakota. He has held both the Golden Glove and North-American boxing titles. Hill was a 1984 Olympic silver medalist and won the World Boxing Association's light heavyweight title from 1987 to 1990.

Roger Maris held the single season home-run record for 37 years.

Thousands of water lovers flock to Lake Sakakawea every summer.

Summertime activities include biking, golf, fishing, and hunting. Lake Sakakawea is popular among water-skiers, boaters, swimmers, and scuba divers. Sun lovers can relax along the lake's 1,600 miles of shoreline. Devils Lake, including Devils Lake State Park, is also a popular area. Lake Metigoshe State Park is a destination for picnickers and campers, while outdoor enthusiasts can see animals and birds at Theodore Roosevelt National Park.

Despite cold, snowy weather, sports continue throughout the winter. Residents can lace up their skates to take part in a hockey game, or go skating on indoor and outdoor rinks. There are also local curling clubs. Others take to the great outdoors on downhill or cross-country skis, snowmobiles, snowshoes, or sleds. Many lakes are open for ice fishing.

QUICK FACTS

North Dakota's largest natural lake is Devils Lake. Its name comes from a legend that tells of many Dakota warriors who once drowned there while returning from battle.

Lake Sakakawea is North Dakota's largest artificial lake. It was formed when Garrison Dam was built across the Missouri River in the 1950s.

The town of Portal is home to an international golf course, stretching from North Dakota into Canada. An international hole-in-one can be scored on the ninth hole. The tee for the ninth hole is in Canada and the cup is in the United States. George Wegener scored the first international hole-in-one in 1934.

The badlands offer many trails for hikers and horseback riders.

North Dakota is home to more than ninety golf courses.

Brain Teasers

1

Why is North Dakota the thirty-ninth state?

Answer: North Dakota is called the thirty-ninth state, and South Dakota the fortieth, but it is not known whether President Benjamin Harrison signed the document for North Dakota or for South Dakota first. The state is only said to be thirty-ninth because it comes first alphabetically.

2

What item did North Dakota's Métis invent?

Answer: The Métis invented the Red River cart, a two-wheeled cart pulled by an ox. It was known for its ability to cross the rough prairie terrain.

3

Why is North Dakota almost always windy?

Answer: Since there are no mountains or forests to stand in the way, the wind blows across the state almost all of the time. This means that there are often summer dust storms and winter blizzards.

4

What items did the Native Peoples trade with early fur traders?

Answer: North Dakota's Native Peoples traded bison hides, meat, and beaver furs in exchange for metal pots, glass beads, cloth, and guns.

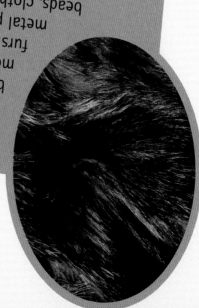

5

What natural disaster resulted in the evacuation of Grand Forks?

Answer: In 1997, the Red River flooded after a winter of heavy snowfall. In Grand Forks alone, almost 90 percent of the residents had to be evacuated, and more than 70 percent of the buildings were damaged.

6

Who were Lewis and Clark?

Answer: Meriwether Lewis and William Clark were explorers sent by the United States government to map unknown parts of the nation. They entered what is now North Dakota in 1804. Over the winter, they built Fort Mandan at the site of the Mandan and the Hidatsa villages.

7

Who says "Only the Best Come North"?

Answer: "Only the Best Come North" is the motto for the Minot Air Force Base.

8

How did Writing Rock State Historic Site get its name?

Answer: The site is called Writing Rock for the petroglyphs carved on to two boulders. The drawings are probably of the Thunderbird, a bird worshipped by the Plains people.

FOR MORE INFORMATION

Books

Aylesworth, Thomas and Virginia. *The Great Plains: Montana, Nebraska, North Dakota, South Dakota, Wyoming.* Discovering America Series. New York: Chelsea House Publishers, 1995.

Herguth, Margaret S. *America the Beautiful: North Dakota.* Chicago: Children's Press, 1990.

Jacobson, Daniel. *The North Central States.* New York: Franklin Watts, 1984.

Web sites

You can also go online and have a look at the following Web sites:

50 States: North Dakota
http://www.50states.com/ndakota.htm

Discover North Dakota
http://discovernd.com

Geobop's North Dakota
http://www.geobop.com/World/NA/US/ND/index.htm

North Dakota Tourism
http://www.ndtourism.com

Some Web sites stay current longer than others. To find other North Dakota Web sites, enter search terms such as "North Dakota," "International Peace Garden," "Turtle Mountain," or any other topic you want to research.

GLOSSARY

albino: an animal or person that lacks normal coloring

appointed: assigned to an office or a position

bearings: machine parts that support other moving parts, usually parts that rotate

decentralized: concentration of power removed from the central government and given to the regional governments

fossil: the remains of a prehistoric plant or animal, usually preserved in rock

geographic: relating to Earth's physical features

homesteading: to settle and farm land, normally under the Homestead Act

humus: organic part of soil made up of decayed vegetable and animal matter

immigrants: people who move to a place from another country

lignite coal: a soft type of coal with wood-like texture

Louisiana Purchase: a large amount of territory purchased from France by the United States in 1803

migrate: seasonal movement of animals

petroglyphs: drawings carved into rock

population density: the average number of people per unit of area

pothole lakes: small, shallow basins left behind by glaciers

powwows: Native-American gatherings, featuring dancing, music, and drumming

precipitation: rain, snow, or hail that falls to the earth's surface

reservations: lands reserved for Native Americans

surveyor: someone who measures land

urban: relating to the city

wetlands: areas of land often filled with water, such as marshes or swamps

INDEX